BOARD GAME TOURNAMENT

VIRGINIA LOH-HAGAN

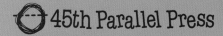
45th Parallel Press

Published in the United States of America by Cherry Lake Publishing
Ann Arbor, Michigan
www.cherrylakepublishing.com

Reading Adviser: Marla Conn MS, Ed., Literacy specialist, Read-Ability, Inc.
Book Designer: Felicia Macheske

Photo Credits: © bobby20/Shutterstock.com, cover, 1; © Mike Flippo/Shutterstock.com, 3; © Orange Line Media/Shutterstock.com, 5; © Tatiana Popova/Shutterstock.com, 7, 30; © karalon/iStock, 9; © oguzdkn/iStock, 10; © Tiplyashina Evgeniya/Shutterstock.com, 11; © Sean MacD/Shutterstock.com, 14; © Pao Laroid/Shutterstock.com, 15; © Lucky Business/Shutterstock.com, 17; © stockyimages/Shutterstock.com, 18; © photka/Shutterstock.com, 18; © PacoRomero/iStock, 20; © PHOTO FUN/Shutterstock.com, 21; © MyImages - Micha/Shutterstock.com, 22, 31 © fstop123/iStock.com, 23; © Nicole Weiss/Shutterstock.com, 25; © LI CHAOSHU/Shutterstock.com, 27; © Bloomicon/Shutterstock.com, 28; © Karramba Production/Shutterstock.com, 28; © Blend Images/Shutterstock.com, 29; © Filip Fuxa/Shutterstock.com, 31; MyImages-Micha/Shutterstock.com, 31; © wavebreakmedia/Shutterstock.com, back cover; © Dora Zett/Shutterstock.com, back cover

Graphic Elements Throughout: © pashabo/Shutterstock.com; © axako/Shutterstock.com; © IreneArt/Shutterstock.com; © Katya Bogina/Shutterstock.com; © Belausava Volha/Shutterstock.com; © Nik Merkulov/Shutterstock.com; © Ya Tshey/Shutterstock.com; © kubais/Shutterstock.com; © Sasha Nazim/Shutterstock.com; © Infomages/Shutterstock.com; © Ursa Major/Shutterstock.com; © topform/Shutterstock.com; © Art'nLera/Shutterstock.com; © Fafarumba/Shutterstock.com

45th Parallel Press is an imprint of Cherry Lake Publishing.

Library of Congress Cataloging-in-Publication Data has been filed and is available at catalog.loc.gov

Cherry Lake Publishing would like to acknowledge the work of The Partnership for 21st Century Skills.
Please visit *www.p21.org* for more information.

Printed in the United States of America
Corporate Graphics

ABOUT THE AUTHOR

Dr. Virginia Loh-Hagan is an author, university professor, former classroom teacher, and curriculum designer. She loves playing board games. She has a closet full of games. Her favorite game is *Innovation*. She lives in San Diego with her very tall husband and very naughty dogs. To learn more about her, visit www.virginialoh.com.

TABLE OF CONTENTS

CHAPTER ONE

WHAT DOES IT MEAN TO HOST A BOARD GAME TOURNAMENT?

Do you love playing games? Do you love solving problems? Do you love competing? Then, starting a board game tournament is the right project for you!

Board games are played on a table. They have game boards. They have game pieces. They have cards. They have rules. They have different playing times. Some games are short. Some games are long. Some are hard. Some are easy.

Some games are based on **strategy**. Strategy means skill. Some games are based on luck. Some games are based on both. Some games have a theme. A theme is a topic. An example is dragons.

Play board games. Learn from board game players.

KNOW THE LINGO

CDG: card-driven game

Crib sheet: cheat sheet, reference card

D6: six-sided die

Downtime: time that a player spends doing nothing while waiting for other players to complete their turns

Dry: boring games

Endgame: the final time period in a game that determines the winner

Expansion: an add-on game that extends the playability

Fart-factor: sound that a game box makes when it closes

Filler: easy and fast game that's played between harder games

Gateway game: easy game used to introduce newbies to board gaming

Kingmaker: a losing player who has the power to decide the winner

Meaty: hard games that require deep thinking

Newbie: new player

RAW: rules as written

RPG: role-playing game

Turtling: playing defensively

Gamers are players. They like playing board games. They are serious about playing. They play a lot. They like winning. They like learning. They like figuring out things.

Some gamers play in board game tournaments. Tournaments are contests. They're a series of many games. Losing gamers are kicked out. Winning gamers move on to the next level. Gamers compete for a big prize. The winner is the champion.

Start a board game tournament whenever you want. They're popular all year long. You'll have fun! You'll meet lots of people. The best part is playing board games.

Attend board game tournaments.

CHAPTER TWO

WHAT DO YOU NEED TO HOST A BOARD GAME TOURNAMENT?

Choose a date.

➡ **Host in the afternoon.**

➡ **Host on a non-school day.**

Choose a place.

➡ **Decide to play indoors or outdoors.**

➡ **Use places available to you. Use places with tables and chairs. Examples are schools, libraries, and parks.**

Choose the type of game. There are many different types.

➡ **Cooperative** games are when players work together. They play against the game.

➡ **Designer games are social strategy games. They're hard to play.**

➡ **Roll-and-move games are family games. They're easy board games.**

➡ **Trivia** games are when players answer questions. Trivia are facts.

➡ **War games are strategy games. They have a military theme.**

➡ **Word games are when players make words.**

Check other events happening at the same time.

Decide the tournament rules.

➡ **Decide who can play. Decide the ages of players.**

➡ **Decide playing time per** round**. A round is a game. Most games take 30 minutes.**

➡ **Decide how players win.**

Choose the type of tournament. There are different types.

➡ **There's single** elimination**. Players are kicked out when they lose. Other players keep playing as long as they're winning. The winner is the undefeated player.**

➡ **There's double elimination. Players can lose two times. Then, they're kicked out.**

➡ **There's round-robin. Each player plays every other player. The player with the most wins is champion.**

Check the playing time on board games.

Get players.

➡ **Consider how many players you need.**

➡ **Consider skill levels. Host different events for different skills. The skill levels are beginner, intermediate, and advanced. Intermediate are good players. Advanced are really good players.**

➡ **Promote the event. Tell everyone.**

➡ **Share how to sign up. Set a deadline.**

➡ **Post a list of games. Require players to know how to play games.**

Get people to help you.

➡ **Hire referees. They make decisions. They say who wins. They say who loses. They handle disagreements. They break ties. Ties are when people have the same score.**

➡ **Get scorekeepers. They keep track of who's winning.**

Get people to help you set up and clean up.

TRY THIS!

Challenge your players. Host a board game mash-up! Encourage people to be creative.

You'll need: two board games, 4 to 8 players, paper, pens

Steps

1 Create teams of 2 to 4 players.

2 Set a time limit. An hour is a good time frame.

3 Give each team two games. (Make sure players have already played the games.)

4 Tell them to create a new game. Have them combine the two games. Allow them to use any pieces from the games.

5 Have each team write down the rules.

6 Plan another event. Allow teams to play the new games. Encourage them to make changes. Encourage them to improve the game.

Get supplies. These are things you'll need.

➡ **Get board games. Get enough games for the players. Make sure you have all the game pieces. Keep extra pieces handy.**

➡ **Make copies of rules. Keep extra copies handy.**

➡ **Get prizes. The best prizes would be new games. Get medals for the winners. Medals are awards.**

➡ **Get tables. Get chairs.**

➡ **Get scoreboards. This is how scores are recorded. They're on a big board. This is for everyone to see.**

➡ **Get a speaker system. This is so you can announce things.**

➡ **Get timers.**

➡ **Get snacks. Get drinks.**

Count game pieces before playing.

CHAPTER THREE

HOW DO YOU SET UP A BOARD GAME TOURNAMENT?

Choose the games. There are options.

➡ **Choose to focus on one game. This is a popular tournament style.**

➡ **Choose to focus on several games. But make sure skill levels are the same for each round.**

Make signs for each game. These signs summarize the game. They provide quick descriptions.

➡ **Include name of each game.**

➡ **Include objective. This is the goal of the game.**

→ Include **mechanics**. This is how players win. These are the main game moves.

→ Provide game rules. This gives more details.

→ Consider hosting an event before the tournament. Let players play the games. Give them time to practice.

→ Choose to focus on several games. But make sure skill levels are the same for each round.

Create a sticker coding system to organize games.

WELLINGTON JIGHERE

Wellington Jighere was born in Nigeria. He's a professional Scrabble player. Scrabble is a board game. Players get points by building words. Jighere won the Scrabble world championship. He played 32 rounds. He's the first African world champion. He focuses on his game. He advises being serious. He said, "You can't afford to waste too much energy doing unnecessary chatter. During a tournament, I see it as business time. And that is no time to be joking around." Thirty of the top 100 best players are from Nigeria. They have a strategy. They play many short words for a lot of points. This also blocks the board.

Create a form for players. Make players submit a form.

➡ **Ask for names.**

➡ **Ask for ages.**

➡ **Ask for contact information. This includes address. This includes phone number.**

➡ **Ask for an emergency contact. This is a person to call if there's trouble. Be prepared.**

Make sure players sign up. They should sign up days before the event.

➡ **Ask players to commit. This means they show up.**

➡ **Make a waiting list. These are people who wanted to sign up. But there wasn't room for them. Put them on this list. Call them if players don't show up.**

➡ **Send players tournament rules.**

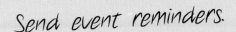

Send event reminders.

Schedule the day's events.

Plan the event.

➡ **Set time for the rounds.**

➡ **Allow time for openers. These are easy games. Players need time before playing. They get ready. They warm up.**

➡ **Allow time for breaks. Players get tired. Give them time to rest.**

➡ **Allow time for closers. Closers are easy games. They give players time to wind down.**

Set up brackets. Brackets show players for each round. They show the winners of each round.

➡ **Set up the first players to play.**

➡ **Match players randomly. This means in no order. You can pick the players out of a hat.**

➡ **After each round, fix the brackets. Do this until there's a champion.**

Consider making money. Tournaments cost money. You can host events to pay for future events. Some people host tournaments to make money. They raise **funds** for causes. Funds are money. Causes are good deeds.

➡ **Charge players to play. This is an entry fee. People pay to play.**

➡ **Sell drinks. People get thirsty. They'll pay for drinks.**

➡ **Sell snacks. People get hungry. They'll pay for snacks.**

➡ **Get someone to handle the money.**

Consider making it a free event.

➡ **Ask players to bring snacks. Ask them to bring drinks. Everyone can share.**

➡ **Ask for donations. This is when people give money.**

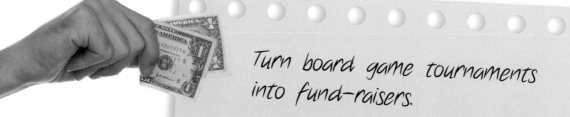

Turn board game tournaments into fund-raisers.

CHAPTER FOUR

HOW DO YOU RUN A BOARD GAME TOURNAMENT?

You've got players. You've got board games. You're ready to host a tournament!

Set up the place.

- ➡ Set up tables.

- ➡ Set up chairs.

- ➡ Set up a place for the games.

- ➡ Set up the snacks and drinks area. Keep away from games. This is to keep games clean.

- ➡ Set up the brackets.

Set up a front table. This is where people sign in.

➡ **Greet people.**

➡ **Give out the rules.**

Set up the board games.

➡ **Put out the game boards.**

➡ **Set up the game pieces.**

➡ **Put signs and rules at each table.**

Download extra copies of game rules from the Internet.

QUICK TIPS

- Learn games before the tournament. Know the rules. Play practice rounds. Be ready to answer questions.

- Learn from each game. Talk about how you played. Talk about mistakes made. Talk about different strategies.

- Learn more about the game's theme.

- Tape the rules to the inside of the box. This keeps rules from getting lost. This keeps rules handy.

- Put game pieces in plastic zipper bags. Don't lose pieces.

- Get fabric softener sheets. Put them inside game boxes. This keeps boxes from smelling musty.

- Place clear tape on box corners. Place clear tape along seams. This keeps boxes from tearing.

- Clean board games with soap and water. Dampen a sponge. Move in a circular motion.

Start the tournament.

- ⇒ Welcome everyone.

- ⇒ Introduce the tournament.

- ⇒ Let players warm up. Let them play openers.

- ⇒ Tell players to introduce themselves to their opponents. Opponents are people you're playing against.

- ⇒ Give players time to decide roles. Give them time to decide game order.

- ⇒ Let the games begin! Start the timers.

Keep track of things.

- ⇒ Walk around. Check on things.

- ⇒ Make sure helpers are where they should be.

- ⇒ Make sure players have what they need.

- ⇒ Keep track of the winners of each round. Update the brackets. Set up the next rounds.

- ⇒ Allow breaks between rounds. Make people get up. Sitting too long is not good.

Take pictures.

Set up the closers.

➡ Have players play closers. Have them play just for fun.

➡ Figure out winners while players wind down.

End the tournament.

➡ Announce the winning player. Announce the players that came in second and third.

➡ Host an awards ceremony. Give out medals. Give out prizes.

➡ Thank the players.

➡ Thank your helpers.

➡ Ask people to come to future events.

➡ Clean up. Don't leave a mess.

➡ Send a note to the players. Thank them again. Ask them to give you **feedback**. Have them tell you what they liked. Have them tell you what you can improve.

Give out medals for best game move.

D.I.Y. EXAMPLE!

STEPS	EXAMPLES
Why	• To have fun • To improve board game strategies
Name	The Not-Boring Board Game Tourney
Place	Community room at local library
Type	Single elimination
Rules	• The games are two-player designer games. • The tournament will start with 16 players. Players can be any age. They should be average to advanced gamers. They must know how to play the games already. • Players keep playing as long as they're winning. The winner is the undefeated player. • Each game can be no longer than 30 minutes.

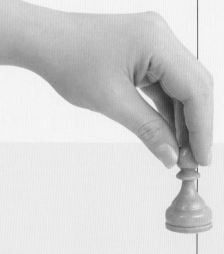

STEPS	EXAMPLES
Rounds	◆ Start with 16 players playing 8 games. Have them play *Ticket to Ride*.
	◆ Winners will play 4 games. Have them play *Forbidden Island*.
	◆ Winners will play 2 games. Have them play *King of Tokyo*.
	◆ Winners will play final game for the championship. Have them play *Innovation*.

GLOSSARY

advanced (uhd-VANSD) a skill level indicating someone is really good; mastery level

brackets (BRAK-its) schedules of players and winners

closers (KLOHZ-urz) easy games played to wind down

cooperative (koh-AH-pur-uh-tiv) working together for a common goal

donations (doh-NAY-shuhnz) gifts

elimination (ih-lim-uh-NAY-shuhn) being kicked out

entry fee (EN-tree FEE) cost of doing something, paying to play

feedback (FEED-bak) information about what people like and what can be improved

funds (FUHNDZ) money

gamers (GAY-murz) people who play board games as a hobby

intermediate (in-tur-MEE-dee-it) a skill level indicating someone is good but still learning

mechanics (muh-KAN-iks) game moves, how one wins a game

openers (OH-puhn-urz) easy games played as warm-ups

opponents (uh-POH-nuhnts) enemies, people you are playing against

randomly (RAN-duhm-lee) not chosen, having no order

referee (ref-uh-REE) someone who makes decisions about a game

round (ROUND) a game in a series of games

strategy (STRAT-ih-jee) skill

ties (TYZ) situations when two people have the same score

tournaments (TOOR-nuh-muhnts) contests

trivia (TRIV-ee-uh) facts and details about various topics

INDEX

LEARN MORE

BOOKS

Blair, Beth L., and Jennifer A. Ericsson. *The Everything Kids' Games and Puzzles Book: Secret Codes, Twisty Mazes, Hidden Pictures, and Lots More—For Hours of Fun!* Avon, MA: Adams Media, 2013.

Morehead, Albert H., and Geoffrey Mott-Smith. *Hoyle's Rules of Games: The Essential Family Guide to Card Games, Board Games, Parlor Games, New Poker Variations, and More.* New York: Signet, 2001.

Swanson, Jennifer. Brain Games: *The Mind-Blowing Science of Your Amazing Brain.* Washington, DC: National Geographic Society, 2015.

WEB SITES

BoardGameGeek: https://boardgamegeek.com

Going Cardboard: A Board Game Documentary: www.boardgamemovie.com

Watch It Played: https://www.youtube.com/user/WatchItPlayed